The Bible and the Law

Many people think of Norman Vincent Peale
Thinking" as the original text on the Law of
popular and powerful teachings of Jerry and Esthei ......,
think of Napolean Hill as the father of the modern day concept.

Any one of those could arguably be considered the modern day origin. One
that is more in tune with the way things are in this day and age, but there are
MANY far earlier text that help us understand what the Law of Attraction
really is. Many of them are well known, and may surprise you… they are
often religious texts and yes, the Bible is one of them.

Still, in spite of the connection the Law of Attraction shares with all of the
concepts of the Bible, Christians are often worried about the practice of it.
They fear they are turning their backs on their faith when nothing could be
further from the truth. You will see in the pages of this book, that the Law of
Attraction is very in tune with the teachings of the Christian Bible.

What is the Law of Attraction?

The Law of Attraction is not a new concept. It has been around for centuries. Only in the last decade has it become a publically taught concept. Perhaps the most well-known book regarding the concept of the law of attraction was "The Power of Positive Thinking" by Normal Vincent Peale.

However, there have been many, many writings dealing with the law of attraction, some dating back to ancient times, and most hidden by those who really didn't want others to know about the power they held within themselves, for any number of reasons. Some people didn't want others to know the secret, because they felt that they would no longer be able to use it for themselves since so many would be asking for things.

The universe/God is unlimited in its power to provide for those that ask.

Some sought to hide the writings regarding such power, because they would lose their position in society. The church (any denomination, but largely Catholic in the early days), is most guilty of this practice. It's not hard to figure out why this happened.

Why would the people in power in the church want the common man to know what he or she is capable of? If everyone knew, understood and really trusted the method, they would no longer need the church.

The church's desire to hide this knowledge is not a new realization. There have been many "councils" where men in power in the church met to decide on what teachings should be used, and what should be discarded, as if they and not the universe/God were in charge of what should be known.

The First Council of Nicea is the most recognized of these meetings, and it was then, when the religion of Christianity was in its relative infancy, that men came together to guarantee their power and to change the world for centuries. Of course, the people that still have the most to lose if this were widely known proclaim this is not the case.

Whether you believe that the council hid truths from the world or not, the one undisputed fact of the council of Nicea is that it adopted the creed determining the relationship of Jesus to God, in being that he was the ONLY son of God. Even if no other subterfuge ever existed, this act alone changed the shape of belief and the tone of the entire text of Jesus' work.

Long before the council, the law of attraction was evident in both religion and writings. Today, very few know about it, and how it relates to them in a spiritual sense. Today, when many look into the teachings of the law of attraction, they are simply looking for a method of getting what they want.

The law of attraction, is at its heart, basically that. There's much more to it, though. The law of attraction is a very spiritual connection that creates gives people back a connection to God. Many Christians have known it in their hearts for all of their lives. They just didn't realize it, because the things the church teaches often conflict with the Law of Attraction for its own gain.

The Law of Attraction has also had its fair share of human frailty to blame for not being revealed and accepted as a truth by many. We don't feel we deserve the things we desire. We don't believe that there is a power out there that will give us what we want. We get sucked into the "hell" that is all around us daily, and it becomes our reality.

Humans make excuses for what they are afraid to accept. When things don't work out on their time table, they excuse it saying it wasn't meant to be, or God said 'No.' But God, the universe, does not say no. Not ever.

It's hard for human beings to accept a concept that they can't control. They can't set a time table for, or make a definitive plan to follow. Of course, that doesn't mean it isn't possible to make plans when trusting in the Law of Attraction, but it does mean that when things happen at the pace the universe/God determines, we need to follow that pace, not our own.

Trust is difficult for people too. Trusting in something that can't be seen, or touched, it is the age-old quandary when considering any concept of God. The reality is, however, that God is really based in science, and it can be determined.

The Energy of the Universe and Our Connection to God

God is all things. All things are made of energy. God is everywhere. Energy is everywhere. The entire universe and everything in it is made up of energy, even us.

We were created in God's image. Does that mean God is a person, a human being? No, that is the misconception that blocks the belief in the all-encompassing God force. People are carbon based atoms driven by an energy field. The very base of our being is energy.

"If you believe in me, you will never die." Did Jesus really mean 'him' alone? Or did he mean "me" in the collective sense of God and the universe, the energy field that is the base of all life? The reality is, you will never die—period.

The body will collapse and die, but the energy that is within you cannot die. It will go on, because it has no choice. Energy cannot die. It MUST go somewhere. That is a scientific fact.

Where does energy go when it is released from the body? Well, it doesn't take much to understand that it will return to the collective energy that is the universe... the energy that is God. So when we die, we return to the God source, to the universe.

What is Energy

When a scientist looks under a microscope everything is an energy field. If asked, a quantum physicist would answer, "What creates the world?" with a single word: Energy.

A basic description of energy is that, it can never be created or destroyed, it always was, always has been, everything that ever existed always exists, it's moving into form, through form and out of form.

That is what is said of "God" as well. Any of the religions, and especially Christianity, say that God created the world. God was not created, he was there in the beginning, and he has no end, he will always be. God is in everything that every existed and will always be a part of everything that exists. It moves into and out of form and through all things.

God IS Energy, and the Universe IS Energy.

Moving Mountains

If you believe, you can move mountains. Most people, even those not particularly religious have heard this biblical reference before. It comes from the New Testament, Mathew 7:20 He replied, "Because you have so little faith. Truly I tell you, if you have faith as small as a mustard seed, you can say to this mountain, 'Move from here to there,' and it will move. Nothing will be impossible for you." (NIV)

This paragraph has a lot of meaning for believers, and it directly relates to the Law of Attraction for which Jesus preached in great length although it wasn't called the Law of Attraction, it was called belief in God.

The main problem for those who read about the Law of Attraction, and start trying to practice the principles of it, or even those who feel they are religious and believe the passage above, is that they ask for what they desire and it doesn't seem to happen.

A popular, modern saying to attribute to the lack of action by God or the universe is "God did answer, and the answer was no."

That seems to, sadly, make sense to most people. It is a way of allowing for a failure while still maintaining belief. However, the fact is that Jesus NEVER says that the answer will be no. He implicitly says if you have faith NOTHING will be impossible. Nothing—absolutely nothing. Not most things. Not, if God thinks it is okay.

NOTHING will be impossible for you. Mark 9:23 says "Everything is possible for him who believes." It doesn't say for him who does good, or when God says it is okay. It says EVERYTHING is possible for him who BELIEVES.

So why don't more people who believe in God and ask for something get it? The final requirement of the Law of Attraction, and of God's biblical word on the matter is found in Luke 17:6 If you have faith as small as a mustard seed, you can say to this tree, be uprooted and planted in the sea and it will obey you.

That clearly shows that FAITH in the truth that the universe/God will give you what you ask is also required, and as human beings, we tend to waiver on that one a lot, or make excuses for it not happening before it has a chance to occur so that we don't look like fools to others. When right under the surface, the change was about to happen, then got shut off by our wavering faith. Faith and belief go hand in hand, but are not the same thing.

Okay, so you may ask why do the things I ask for not come true?

First, you must really be sure of the things you are asking for. If you think about the popular saying "Be careful what you wish for, it may come true," you can see that sometimes, the things we think we might actually end up being a nightmare.

The universe/God does not simply blink and make things happen immediately for a reason. If it did, the minute you thought about a desire, it would appear. The world would be a pretty wild place if every time someone thought about something they thought was cool, or would be a good way to live, it happened. Paradigms would be shifting everywhere, and there would always be those "instant nightmares." Thinking about a crocodile could make one appear in front of you at any given moment.

The universe/God, gives a desire time to become a solid concept in your mind, and you need to truly think about it in all aspects to be sure it is really what you want.

Second: In this modern, technological age, we are really used to immediate response. We want things to happen immediately. We expect instant gratification. Have you ever really looked at a mountain before? Stood next to one. Touched it. Gave it a shove? A mountain is a pretty big thing to move. It's going to take a little time.

When you truly want something, believe in it, can envision it, the universe/God WILL make it happen. Now, sometimes what you want will happen immediately—those are the times people happily quote the above biblical reference so everyone can believe in the truth. Those are also the times when followers of the Law of Attraction happily point out how easy it is to bring about changes in your own reality.

In a great many cases, however, making the changes necessary to alter a reality take a little time. Otherwise, like in the explanation above, shifts would be so disrupting as to be almost horrific, both to the person getting the desire, and to everyone around. Instant gratification of large changes also doesn't leave any time to make sure the desire is going to really be the chosen outcome, or even a happy temporary situation.

Case in point: A few years ago, living in a rural area, I decided I wanted to move back to the city close to where I had grown up. I thought about it all the time. Then a situation arose after about a year, where a family member's home became available and my husband and I could have it for free. Sounded great, but there were a few obstacles in the way. I constantly thought about it though, and put it in my mind. Less than a year later I was living there with my family. I didn't think about the fact that the house may not be up to par.

I should have. I learned an important lesson.

Think about the desire, but make sure you keep an open mind about exact situations. I have a new dream, and it is constantly in my mind, but I have the qualification of: a house like this, this one specifically IF it is in good condition and acceptable in all ways that fit the all around dream situation.

The permanence of mountains: Even though mountains are big, formidable and hard to move, they are moveable. This is helpful in getting the desires you want, even when they are seemingly as big and hard to get as a mountain, but also in allowing for a change when desires shift as well. You don't have to feel like, well, this is what I wished for, so this is what I get.

This feeling spawned another "settling for it" phrase: You made your bed, now you have to sleep in it. No you don't. Not for long anyway. You may have to deal with the situation you desired until the new one formulates, but that's it. You can change your desires, and you can expect that new dream to materialize. There is no limit to how many times you can make a request of the universe/God. It is never ending just as God and the universe are never-ending.

Case in point: I have always loved water. About four years ago I decided I really wanted a boat. Not just any boat, a good sized cruiser. Well, in less than a year, I had just that. A really nice, 25 foot cabin cruiser. We really loved it, but there were some things that could have been better/different. It wasn't that the boat was bad. It wasn't. It was that, never having had a boat before, I had made a few mistakes in my requests.

So I changed them. I decided that a smaller, trailerable boat just for fishing, a bass boat was my new dream. Got it. It took about two years after I changed my request to make it happen, but it happened. We really enjoy the bass boat, but it isn't everything I really want. More specifically, it's great for what it does, and I don't really want to get rid of it, but I want something more, so my request has changed.

This new request is very recent, so I don't expect it to happen overnight. In fact, since my new request is tied to a major life change in location and housing as well, I expect it will take a year or two to happen... I definitely believe it will happen however.

It's not wrong to change desires as your needs or wants change. There is no limit. Nowhere in scripture does Jesus say ask and you will receive --- within limits. Nope. It's simply: ask and ye shall receive.

In John 6:24 it says: Until now you have not asked for anything in my name. Ask and you will receive, and your joy will be complete. (NIV)

One of the first things most people have to do when starting to practice the law of attraction is to realize that making changes is not up to them. Your job is to ask. It is the universe/God's job to create the changes required for it to happen. However, there is a catch—sometimes.

It is your job to take advantage of the opportunities that the universe/God puts in front of you. Sometimes the request you make will take no action on your part at all Sometimes the gift given will require a change of placement or situation. Sometimes that opportunity takes the form of work. That's the one that often gets overlooked.

Most of the time, the answer to your prayer need only be recognized and accepted.

There's an old joke about a man drowning in the ocean, praying to God for help, and a cruise ship goes by and he waves them off, saying no thanks, God will rescue me. Another goes by and tries to help the man who waves them off too, saying God is going to save him. And God is looking down thinking "how many times do I have to send someone to save that man before he accepts my help?"

The universe/God probably asks the same question about people he is trying to grant a desire to in answer to their prayer. "How many times do I have to offer this guy his dream before he reaches out and grabs it?"

The second hardest thing for most people to accept is that there are no limits even in a limited situation. We get hung up on our current work/environment, and think that if there is no way our jobs can provide the money required, or our ability is limited, or the environment we live in is unsuitable to making the changes necessary that it won't be possible to achieve the dream we want, even if we think the law of attraction is real.

It is not up to YOU to make the changes happen. It is up to the universe/God to make those changes happen, and it will happen. It isn't up to you to figure out how. It is only up to you to ask and believe.

The inability to accept that there are no limits to the universe/God's power to provide the thing we want makes us limit our request. I want a beautiful, modern, up to date home… but that's expensive, so maybe I'll just ask for a different house. I want the home to be in this state, but that's too far away, and the houses are too expensive there, so I'll just say somewhere else.

Non-specific requests are dangerous to the ability of the law of attraction for two reasons. First, it creates a sort of hodge podge of desires that ends up not being a desire at all. There is no real request, and when it is discernible, the end result may not be what you wanted at all to begin with. The second reason such limits and bargaining hurt the ability of the universe/God to provide, is that the person making the request doesn't really believe it can happen, and it's a half-hearted request.

Bargaining is another method of "cheating" what people think is asking for too much. They don't want to seem greedy after all. Since greed is a "sin," they feel guilty about asking for something they consider to be a big request, and they make deals with the universe/God in order to make it seem like a better deal all around. You can't give the universe/God anything it doesn't already have.

That doesn't mean that you don't have to be a good person, help others when you are able. Quite the opposite, those acts, when committed in a genuine manner are what helps you stay in tune with the universe/God. It means that saying you will do something like give money to charity, help the less fortunate, or whatever the bargain is for getting what you desire, is both disingenuous, and not even remotely necessary. The universe/God does not say ask and if you are good enough I'll give it to you. It says ask, and you will receive.

The Power of Belief

Proverbs 23:7 *For as he thinketh in his heart, so is he.*

This has a two-sided meaning, both equally pertinent to the teachings of the bible regarding our place in the universe and to God. First, the most commonly held meaning by traditional churches, in that if you are good at heart, and seek to do good things, you will be a good person. The Law of Attraction also demands that we be good at heart, not seeking to do harm to others. However, there is a more direct meaning behind this quote in the bible as it pertains to the Law of Attraction. What you believe and think about deep down in your soul, really and truly care about, and want, will be. It will be who you are and what you get out of life in all ways.

In Romans 12:2 the Proverbs 23:7 thought is brought into more clarity: *And be not conformed to this world, but be ye transformed by the renewing of your mind, that ye may prove what is good and acceptable and is the perfect will of God.*

Money is Evil

No, money is not evil. There are a myriad of references to riches in the bible associated with believers.

Proverbs 8:18 *With me are riches and honor, enduring wealth and prosperity.* (NIV)

Philippians 4:19 *And this same God who takes care of me will supply all your needs from his glorious riches, which have been given to us in Christ Jesus.* (NLT)

Psalm 112:3 *Wealth and riches are in their houses, and their righteousness endures forever.* (NIV)

What is "evil" is trusting only in money, not in belief for your happiness. Using money to hurt others is another way that money is evil.

While Jesus said to his disciples, *"Truly I tell you, it is hard for someone who is rich to enter the kingdom of heaven."* In Matthew 19:23 (NIV) the reference is not specifically to the evil of money, or that we should not desire to be rich in all ways including monetarily, it means that having money can lead to corruption and forgetting to believe in the power of the universe/God instead of in the power of money.

People who have money forget to praise the universe/God for their wealth, and forget to connect to the universe/God for their desires. It is also common for people with money to not think about how their money/power can hurt others. However, there are many very philanthropic wealthy people who have learned the important lessons of care and giving through their wealth, and also practice in some form the Law of Attraction in one of its many incarnations.

Matthew 5:3 *"God blesses those who are poor and realize their need for him, for the Kingdom of Heaven is theirs."* Realize that this isn't saying money is bad. It is saying that people who are struggling are reaching and searching for God, they realize they need God. The important thing to realize is that when the universe/God grants your wishes, you STILL need it/him. You still need to be thankful every day for the blessings given to you.

Remember that the Law of Attraction does not just work for bringing about changes in lifestyles or money, it brings a "karma-like" reality as well. *What you attract you receive.* This can be bad as well as good, so it is very important to maintain a positive and gracious manner. This is very rooted in biblical ideology as well.

Where is Heaven

Luke 17:20-21 *Once, on being asked by the Pharisees when the kingdom of God would come, Jesus replied, "The coming of the kingdom of God is not something that can be observed, nor will people say, 'Here it is,' or 'There it is,' because the kingdom of God is in your midst.* (NIV)

Like most people, I'm guilty from time to time and at various points in my life, of thinking of heaven as a place somewhere in the sky. There is a basis for that feeling in that the universe is also somewhere out in space, but it is also everywhere around us, and since we are a part of it, it also exists in each one of us.

Heaven is a complete and total communion with the universe/God. Life itself can be quite heavenly, no matter what your particular situation is. It depends on how you feel about it, think about it, and act within it. The polar opposite is hell. Hell is separation from the universe/God, and it exists as much in our thoughts as in any reality of place.

The Triune God

As Christians we are taught to believe that God is 3 in 1: Father, Son and Holy Ghost. This concept still remains with the Law of Attraction. The energy that comprises the entire Universe, from which all things come=God, the energy that is a part of the Universe that exist inside each individual living thing=the Son, and the power that surrounds us all, constantly moving through us, back to the source and back to us, is the Holy Ghost.

In God's Image

A lot of people fight the idea of our being God-like, and fight even harder to think that the universe equals God. Both concepts are easily supported in scripture however.

In the Bible it says that God made man in his image, but that doesn't mean the physical form. After all, God can't look like every single human on earth. That's what makes the whole, God is white, God is black, Arabic, Jewish, and on and on, silly. God is all and everything.

Man does exist in God's image, because we are a part of God. The REAL part of us, the inner energy, the soul, that is God's image. It isn't black, white, yellow, red, tan or any race or religion. God is pure energy and power.

The Laws of God and the Law of Attraction

Throughout time, the universe/God has reached out to us to help us understand our connection to it, gain a closeness, and achieve all that we desire. Like the old Army motto: Be all that you can be," that is the universe's greatest gift that we can be all that we can be, and want to be. There's no catch to it at all.

Long before any formal rules were written down, the universe/God allowed nature to take its course. Early man followed the instincts that were clear to them in their more natural state. As human beings developed and gained knowledge, one could liken that to the Garden of Eden and the ensuing eating of the tree of knowledge, our minds became clouded. Our own intelligence often gets in the way of our connection to the source of our existence. After that, it became a struggle for the universe/God to achieve a connection to us, and vice versa.

The universe/God has two main ways of communicating with us, the first and what should be the strongest, but often is less attuned to what is being said, is that small voice we all have inside of us. The second is by finding a conduit that has a good connection to that voice, and using them as a mouthpiece. There have been many mouthpieces throughout history, doing the work of the universe/God to communicate and bring us closer to it. Jesus was one of these, and by most accounts, one of the most powerful and longest lasting.

Is it blasphemy to say that Jesus was a man who was a conduit of God, not the only son of God? I don't think so. People think that because Jesus pointed to himself and said: *I am the truth; follow me* (John 10:30), that it means he is the only one who has the truth. It does not say that. Jesus knew the truth, however, and knew most people were blinded to it, so he said listen I am the truth, follow what I am doing. People think that because he said that *he and the Father were one* (John 10:30), that meant only he had that connection.

It is human nature to be self-effacing. In fact, there have been no other prophets throughout history who proclaimed to have a direct connection to God, or to be a true son of God. Allah, Brahma, Abraham, Moses, Muhammad, Socrates, Buddha, none of them proclaimed to be God in whatever name they used for the universe... only Jesus.

For us, that seemed to mean that only Jesus had that connection. Really, however, it was only Jesus that voiced the connection we all have in the way that said look, this is the truth, I and the Father are one. There is another famously difficult verse that is translated slightly differently in the many versions of the text: the kingdom of God is within you.

That is a bold statement, and even that one single phrase is just a little different in each area, but if it is considered from the universe/God point of view, they are all the same and mean the same thing: God is within all of us, not out in space somewhere, disconnected from us.

In Luke 17:21 it says:

New International Version

Nor will people say, 'Here it is,' or 'There it is,' because the kingdom of God is in your midst.

New Living Translation

You won't be able to say, 'Here it is!' or 'It's over there!' For the Kingdom of God is already among you.

English Standard Version

Nor will they say, 'Look, here it is!' or 'There!' for behold, the kingdom of God is in the midst of you.

New American Standard Bible

Nor will they say, 'Look, here it is!' or, 'There it is!' For behold, the kingdom of God is in your midst.

King James Bible

Neither shall they say, Lo here! or, lo there! for, behold, the kingdom of God is within you.

Holman Christian Standard Bible

No one will say, 'Look here!' or 'There!' For you see, the kingdom of God is among you.

Even though none of the prophets before or since Jesus said they were one with God, they all basically say the same thing in different ways, the basic human frailty of feeling less than important, humility based in doubt rather than based in gratification kept them from saying God is right here, and pointing to the inner being.

Be humble before the Lord your God. That is a basic truth present in most religious, and definitely in Christianity. Humility is important, but not humility based on doubt or self-defeating inadequacy. Rather, humility based on being grateful and happy to be a part of a bigger source of energy. Acknowledging that the universe/God is all encompassing and all powerful, and that we are but a small piece of the whole.

Yes, the universe/God does want to be acknowledged and for us to understand that it is it that has the power to change all things, not us on our own. Forgetting that one simple truth is one of the main causes of our being cut off from the universe/God, not by its doing, but by our own feeling of doing everything ourselves. We effectively cut ourself off from the universe/God—and THAT is the truest explanation of hell.

Regardless of who he used to convey the message, the universe/God has reached out to us in many ways to convey the truth to us, and help us live in a way that would bring us closer to it.

Finally, in the end, he sent the message, through Jesus, that the only commandment was to love God. If you truly understand the universe/God, and that God is within you AND everyone around you, there is no way you can break any commandment or law previously spoken.

The Power of Two/ The Power of the Church

In this text, the Church is not the organization, or set of organizations throughout history known as the Church. When Jesus said the Church is the body of Christ, he was simply pointing out that you are your own Church. However, he also pointed out that whenever two or more of you are gathered in his name he will be there.

So why, if we are so connected do we need others? Technically we don't. In fact, Jesus told us to pray in private, not make a public spectacle of our dealings with the universe/God. However, it also makes sense that he said gathering more than one together will make the prayers more powerful. The reasoning is simple enough. More people together means more concentrated energy.

There are two basic reasons this is an effective way to bring prayers to the universe/God. The first is that as stated in the above paragraph, the message to the universe/God will be stronger and swifter because there is more energy involved in the request. The second is a belief factor. This is why even silent prayer circles where no oral request is made, but simply a "pray for him/her" is requested. The one who is praying for a specific thing feels more empowered, and believes more strongly that their prayer is being heard. Since belief is a major factor in the Law of Attraction it helps.

The reality is that it isn't a necessity, so if you don't belong to prayer groups, or want to broadcast your desire to everyone publically, you are not without hope. You are just as strong as long as your belief is just as strong.

Nowhere in the Bible does it say that the Church is a group of people that gathers together to listen to some other human draw their own conclusions from the Word of God and then take collections, or that collections, confessions or other forms of guilt offerings are what it is all about. In fact, Jesus himself was pretty upset at the Sadducees and other "Church" monetization of the day back then. He'd probably be furious now.

There's another reason the two or more teaching is important. We are all connected and normally crave that connection. It is what drives us to make bonds with each other, to develop relationships, and to crave intimacy. It's the reason touching someone we love feels good, it's the reason kissing, what would otherwise be a rather gross behavior, feels so electrifying. It merges our energies.

Everyone has energy inside themselves, but that energy flows freely all around us. It is the concept behind the idea of "my space." You'll hear people say not to "invade their space," and it is immediately understandable without anyone drawing a figure to represent what they mean by that space. However, the concept of not connecting is, or should be, as foreign to us as not breathing. Our doubts, fears and lack of understanding breeds the idea that we should have a private space and not desire others to reach out and touch us in any way unless we are familiar with them AND invite it.

Stumbling Blocks

Doubt is our biggest stumbling block. Not such doubt that the Law of Attraction is real, that our connection to the universe/God is real, or that God actually exists as the universe. That is a part of the doubt, but there's a bigger doubt that exists, the one that says even if God is out there, even if the universe and God are one, and all around us, we can't be a part of that. There's also fear. Fear that we aren't good enough and an even bigger fear, the fear that what we want won't be as good as it seems after all.

While becoming a part of the universe and using the law of attraction usually is a positive experience, in some cases it in itself can cause a darkness that is a pitfall.

Because the Law of Attraction works on a basis of belief and the "rules" as it were, of the law say if it isn't working it is because you don't believe strongly enough, it can become a stumbling block for you, and worse a negative darkness that overshadows your entire life.

Remember that there is no failure. Try not to set time limits. Occasionally some teachers suggest that you make time requests such as "I will have $1,000 by the end of the week" or something along those lines. This can be a catch 22.

If it works in that time period, wow, fantastic right? Sure. Then you can build on the belief of the power. The problem happens when it doesn't materialize in that particular time frame. Maybe it would have taken 8 days, or 2 weeks. Maybe you quit right before the breakthrough.

Sometimes, your own mind says you are tempting the universe and making it prove itself, and that's bad, and you can't have that. So it stops the process. Once you have an experience like that it can shake your belief system. Some people have something small happen like that but keep going bravely only to see more and more failure of the system. It really isn't the system. It is the repetitive failures building on itself in their minds causing a building negativity.

There is still good news! Even if this has happened to you already, all you have to do is recognize it, stop it, and begin again. There is NO failure except quitting.

How to Achieve a State of Attraction

At its most basic, the Law of Attraction is the simplest thing:

- · Ask
- · Believe
- · Receive

Just like the Bible says it should be between us and God. Of course, the actual practice takes a little more work. It is still really just as easy, but we have to train ourselves to do it.

First, it is important to clear the mind of all negative feelings, randomness and scattered thought. In Psalms it says:

"Be still, and know that I am God; I will be exalted among the nations, I will be exalted in the earth." (Psalm 46:10 NIV)

Give yourself a peaceful, quiet place to communicate with the Universe/God. In Matthew it tells us:

But when you pray, go into your room, close the door and pray to your Father, who is unseen. Then your Father, who sees what is done in secret, will reward you. (Matthew 6:6)

Always remember to be thankful. Spend more of your time meditating on the good things in your life. Thanking the Universe/God for the greatness in your life, and all of his generosity. In Psalms it tells us:

Praise the LORD. Give thanks to the LORD, for he is good; his love endures forever. (Psalm 106:1 NIV)

Know that you are not the one doing the giving or creating. No matter what devices the universe/God puts before you to allow the dreams and desires you have to come true, and how hard you work to make use of them, EVERYTHING is possible because of the universe/God. It is easy to lose humility.

People often start off thankful. They recognize the great gift of opportunity, and scream hallelujah, and then soon, as they work at the opportunity and it becomes more and more a job they do to get what they want in the end... they only see them, not the creator's gift.

Achieving your bliss, your completely true state of mind that will allow you to accomplish all that you desire is both extremely easy, and extremely difficult. It is easy because there are no requirements of place, finance or specialty items needed. It is extremely difficult because it requires you to remain consistent in your belief and to fight off the "devil".

So what is the devil, and is it a real entity. The devil is as real as God in that it is a negative force created by the level of negativity in the environment around you. It is also that nagging voice that tells you everything you believe is silly, superstitious (as if that same voice wouldn't fall into the same category when you think about it).

Historical Quotes Relating to the Law of Attraction

Franklin D. Roosevelt.

Men are not prisoners of fate, but only prisoners of their own minds. –

Ralph Waldo Emerson

The secret is the answer to all that has been all this is and all that will be.

Gandhi

Be the change you wish to see in the world.

Henry Ford

Whether you think you can or can't either way you are right.

Winston Churchill

You create your own universe as you go along.

Martin Luther King Jr

Take the first step in faith you don't have to see the whole staircase just take the first step.

Buddha

All that we are is the result of what we have thought.

Alexander Graham Bell

What power this is I cannot say. All that I know is that it exists.

Jesus

It is done unto you as you believe...

Napoleon Hill

Whatever your mind can conceive and can believe, it can achieve.

Albert Schweitzer

Man must cease attributing his problems to his environment, and learn again to exercise his will - his personal responsibility.

Andrew Carnegie

I am no longer cursed by poverty because I took possession of my own mind, and that mind has yielded me every material thing I want, and much more than I need. But this power of mind is a universal one, available to the humblest person as it is to the greatest.

Albert Einstein

Imagination is everything. It is the preview of life's coming attractions.

William James

The greatest discovery of my generation is that human beings can alter their lives by altering their attitudes of mind.

Wayne Dyer

I will see it when I believe it.

John Demartini

Whatever we think about and thank about we bring about.

Robert Collier

All power is from within and is therefore under our control.

Max Planck

All matter originates and exists only by virtue of a force... We must assume behind this force the existence of a conscious and intelligent Mind. This Mind is the matrix of all matter.

The Image of God

Are we the image of God, or are we God himself? Who is God? Where is God? What is God? These are age-old questions that are actually a lot simpler than most of us make them. The biggest problem encountered when trying to come to grips with our relationship with God is the passage from the Bible proclaiming that man was made in the image of God. It is the word "image."

We are sticklers for the visual idea of "image." But image can mean a lot more than physical appearance. After all, if God looks like us, or rather we "look" like God, what exactly is that: black, white, red, yellow, tall, short, thin, fat, American, Japanese, Indian, Arabic, Jew? Is God Jewish just because Jesus was Jewish? What about Mohammed, Buddha?

God is not some old bearded man sitting in the clouds with a naughty and nice list. Somehow we have that image confused with Santa Claus. God is nothing physical at all. Physical is temporary. God is eternal and everlasting. So if God is not physical, and never dies, what about us can be said to be God-like?

Our soul, but what is that exactly? Is it something we can put a finger on? It must be something "real" and "tangible" in the sense that it can be experienced. The only part of us that can never die and isn't reliant on the physical being to survive is the energy that is at the very basis of our composition. Like everything in the universe, we are energy.

There's More to Christianity

Christianity is a roadmap to a "good" and decent, morale life. It is an important aspect of living. It isn't necessary to throw out one in order to have the other. The Law of Attraction is the inner concept of Christianity and the power we all have inside of us. It is taught all through the Bible, the big difference is semantics: remember Shakespeare's famous quote—"a rose by any other name would smell just as sweet." What you call something isn't as important as what it is.

Christianity as a whole, however, incorporates the concepts of how to treat others. In some ways so does the Law of Attraction. You can't have negative feelings or desires and hope to make a positive connection with the universe. You need to be happy for the success of others, treat others well, and really, live up to Jesus' singularly most powerful statement: of all the commandments, this is the one is above all else: love one another.

If we love one another, we cannot break any commandment! None! It is impossible, and if we love one another, we are in tune with the power of positive attraction.